T
LOVE

D1353355

To ....

From ....

First published in Great Britain in 2003
by Egmont Books Limited
239 Kensington High Street, London, W8 6SA

ISBN 0 4052 0492 X

1 3 5 7 9 10 8 6 4 2

Printed in China

The secrets of love ... revealed!
An invaluable book packed full of
inside information, top tips and
fascinating facts on love. Never be
tongue-tied, mystified or terrified again!

First of all, what do they really mean?

Your beloved's handwriting can say a lot about them.

Why not try reading between the lines? It could tell you more than you'd bargained for!

MR FORWARD

Does his writing slant forwards?

This could mean he is brash and headstrong.

**He often charges ahead without
thinking things through.**

This person could be hot-headed,
and get himself into scrapes aplenty!

If this is the one for you, then make sure
he feels in control - no need to tell him
that it's really you in the driving seat, right?

THE BIG
LOOPER

Outgoing and confident,
a happy-go-lucky kind of person.

He's the life and soul of the party,
and may be looking for that special
someone to have fun with.

A Big Looper can be a great person to go out
with, but sometimes the pace can be too much!

Remember - if you're a party animal too,
then this could be a match made in Heaven.

But if all you want is a nice evening in front
of the TV with a take-away, stay clear!

Watch out, there's a spider about!
Is his handwriting so messy you can hardly
read it? Hmm - this could mean the
writer's erratic and unreliable.

Scrambled handwriting can mean you'll
always be kept waiting outside the cinema
and have your birthday forgotten!

But untidy handwriting can also mean
he's intelligent and creative - too busy having
great ideas to write things down properly!

It's a mixed blessing, so if he's really cute,
tell him to pull his socks up, mind his
p's and q's and smarten up his r's.

love you | love you | love you | love you | love you
love you | love you | love you | love you |
u | love you | love you | love you | love you
love you | love you | love you | love you |
u | love you | love you | love you | love you
love you | love you | love you | love you |
u | love you | love you | love you | love you
love you | love you | love you | love you |
u | love you | love you | love you | love you
love you | love you | love you | love you |
u | love you | love you | love you | love you
love you | love you | love you | love you |
u | love you | love you | love you | love you
love you | love you | love you |
u | love you | love you | love
love you | love you | love you
u | love you | love you | love
love you | love you | love you
u | love you | love you | love you | love you
love you | love you | love you | love you

NEAT AND TIDY

Everyone likes neat handwriting (except doctors), but is his handwriting too tidy? And is it really, really small? Do you need a microscope to read his small print?

Tiny, neat handwriting could mean the writer is close-mouthed and tight-fisted!

Over-tidiness can often be an indication of someone who keeps things close to their chest.

Your dream date may well end up as a staring contest . . . with you footing the bill!

Elvis Presley fan Eileen Markovitz keeps sending Valentine's cards to her idol, even though he's been dead since 1977!

California-born Eileen, who changed her name to Eileen-Elvis Presley, has been sending a card every year for 25 years, but The King hasn't written back once! You Ain't Nothin' But A Hound Dog, Elvis! All poor Eileen ever got was a stamp saying Return To Sender!

In 1981, mountaineer **Kit Hardy**
discovered a note inside an envelope
made from scraps of cloth.

What's so weird about that?
Well, Kit was at the top of the world's
second-largest mountain, K2, at the time -
25,000 feet above sea level! The mysterious
note simply said, 'Carry this with you for ever,
All my love, Txx'. Despite a long search
afterwards, Kit never discovered who 'T' was
or what had happened to the bearer of the note.

In 1992, New Yorker Dan Rider proposed to his girlfriend Sherry – using sky-writing!

Romantic Dan hired the plane to fly over her house one Saturday afternoon and pop the question. The vintage biplane soared above Sherry's home, spewing out smoke. 'It went OK until it had to spell her surname, which was Papadimitriou,' laughed Dan. 'The plane ran out of smoke halfway through!' Fortunately Sherry got the message, and they tied the knot four months later at their local airport!

The greatest number of love letters ever sent to someone was 4,000 from lovesick Victor Aziz to his sweetheart Lorna Chapelle.

Parisian baker Victor spent the best part of six years sending cards, notes, letters and gifts to the indifferent Lorna, who never replied to a single one of them. 'I always thought I'd wear her down,' said Victor, optimistically. But it wasn't to be. Lorna eventually married Michel Le Gros who worked for the Post Office!

C'est la vie!

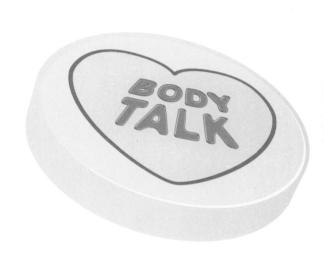

Actions speak louder than words

Sometimes, a person's body language
can give away more secrets than their
so-called best friend! Check out the boys
when they're talking to you. Look out
for those subtle signs - maybe they're
'saying' more than they think!

Are his arms folded,
or is he holding his wrist
with his opposite hand?

He's uncomfortable and feels a little awkward - he's unconsciously giving himself a hug!

He's being shy and protecting himself, so show him there's nothing to be afraid of! Smile loads to let him know he's doing just fine!

Is he touching his nose,
pulling at his ear, and looking
down and to the left? Is he
avoiding looking you in the eye?

Touching or covering his face means unconsciously he could be trying to hide a lie. And not making eye contact is always a dead giveaway!

Don't believe everything he tells you. He may be very convincing, but you have to accept he might not actually be Robbie Williams' best mate after all.

Is he copying you? Is he
sitting with his legs crossed
when you are too? Is he tilting
his head to one side just like
you are? Is it like looking in a mirror?

Copying someone's body language is a sure
signal they're interested. Well done you
- you've got him hooked at last!

Mission accomplished! You're doing fine!
Give yourself a pat on the back.

Singing loudly with both hands
clasped firmly over his ears and his
eyes shut. La-la-la . . . not listening!

WHY?

The subtle signs of
body language
indicate he's not
interested. Trust me.

LATER

You'll probably want
to leave at this point
anyway - that's a
really good instinct.

Next step

Right. You've done your homework.
Now it's time to meet up for a date.
Here are some suggestions of
interesting and exciting things to do . . .

The Cinema

The cinema's an excellent choice for a first date, but make sure you think carefully about what kind of movie you are going to see. Remember - choose wisely!

Scary: This is good! There will be lots of chances for him to comfort you during the really scary bits! But make sure it's not too frightening - running out of the cinema shrieking is unlikely to get a very good response!

Romantic comedy: If he chooses this, it means he's trying to impress you. Ace - you already know you're in with a chance! Either that, or he's completely fixated with Cameron Diaz!

Action: An action movie is a great idea. If you can sit through all those explosions, he'll be dead impressed. Just make sure you know your Arnie from your elbow, otherwise he'll catch you out!

Ice Skating

Bit of a mixed bag.
It's healthy and keeps
you fit. Then again,
you'll probably spend
most of the date
sprawled out on the
ice - not so cool. Best
to avoid this - unless
you think you are the
next Torvill and Dean.

The Mall

Lots of fun stuff to do like shopping, eating
and people-watching. Horrendous possibility
that your dad will turn up doing his shopping:
'Coo-ee! How's Daddy's little princess?' Arrgh!

A false moustache may help you to
disguise yourself from your dad.
However, it may put your date off.

Bowling

You can pretend your beloved is a great bowler, and butter him up: 'Wow – you're really good at this!' Once you've flattered him, he'll be in the palm of your hand.

- dropping the ball on your foot
- not scoring a single point
- not letting go of the ball and ending up trapped in the pin-collecting machine at the end of the lane

 The date's about having fun, not winning, so just relax and enjoy it.

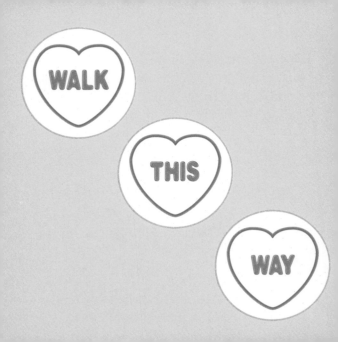

Take a walk

How about simply slipping on your walking
shoes and getting out into the fresh air? After all,
it's free and all that exercise will keep you fit.
But remember - take an umbrella and some
plasters for blisters just in case!

Preparation

Always be realistic. If you need your glasses,
wear them! Glasses are cool these days, falling
over and walking into doors simply isn't!

GOOD

REMEMBER You've got specs appeal!

When preparing for that terrifying first date, pick out your wardrobe carefully. Then just stick with your very first choice. On no account try sixteen other outfits on in a mad panic.

You know why? Well, you'll only end up choosing your original one after all. No one knows why this happens - it's just one of life's great mysteries that's all! Save your energy.

On no account invite your friends along to the date. It might seem like a nice idea having them 'hidden' in the background as moral support, but it'll unsettle your beloved. Remember – no one's at their best when they're surrounded by a pack of giggling mates.

Above all, relax! Don't worry!
Of course, it could turn out to
be the most stomach-fluttering,
joyous day of your life, but then again . . .
Just try not to think about it too much.

If at first you don't succeed!

When 1940's movie star Lauren Bacall
first met Humphrey Bogart, she called him
'a grumpy, funny-looking guy. He looks like
a half-chewed candy bar'. This didn't stop Bogie.
He bombarded her with flowers until she agreed
to go out with him. And his persistence paid off
- they fell in love and got married in 1945!

Don't try too hard!

Dare-devil skier Gerald Luckwitz fell from a ski-lift in Aspen, USA in 1981 and wasn't discovered for four days. Gerald was trying to leap across to another chair to impress some ladies. However, he slipped and fell thirty feet into heavy woods, breaking both ankles and an arm. 'I kept thinking those girls would raise the alarm,' the chastened Romeo said from his hospital bed, 'but they didn't.'

If at first

In 1992, Marshall Fairweather
and Nicola Patterson were married
in New York, USA – a mere 62 years
after they first met. Nicola, aged 84,
said, 'It took me all this time to convince
him. I've proposed to him eight times,
and finally he's agreed!' Bless!

Like a prayer

The patron saint of love is, of course,
St Valentine. But if you are hoping
your date will present you with a huge
bouquet of flowers, perhaps you should
say a prayer or two to St Dorothy -
the patron saint of florists!

And they call it hippo love

Stage magician, Anton Rebard, should have
stuck to card tricks. In 1992, the Swiss
conjurer hypnotised a member of his
audience in Zurich into believing she loved
a stuffed toy animal. The only trouble was,
he couldn't reverse it! The unfortunate
woman spent two days refusing to be parted
from her beloved 'Mr Hippo', insisting they
would live together in the Limpopo river -
then sued Rebard for thousands of pounds
when she was cured! 'Mr Hippo' was said
to be heartbroken too!